Les apprêts d'un déjeuner rustique by Henri-Horace Roland de la Porte circa 1760. (Source: Louvre, Paris)

Normandy Stoneware
Traditional Jersey Pottery

First published in Great Britain
in 2019 by Société Jersiaise
www.societe-jersiaise.org

Copyright (C) 2019 text Margaret Finlaison
Copyright (C) 2019 images and illustrations as credited

A catalogue record of this report is available from the British Library

All rights reserved. No part of this publication may be reproduced, stored in a retrieval system, or transmitted, in any form or by any means, without the prior permission of the publisher. The book is sold subject to the conditions that it shall not, by way of trade or otherwise, be lent, resold, hired out or otherwise circulated without the publisher's prior consent in any form of binding or cover other than that in which it is published and without similar condition being imposed on the subsequent publisher.

ISBN 978 0 901897 98 5

Contents

Normandy Stoneware: An Introduction   7
   Normandy Pottery   7
   The Nature of Stoneware   7
   A History of Production   7
   The Appearance of the Pottery   9
   Pottery Marks and Stamps   9
      Stamped Initials   9
      Stamped Patterns   9
   Dating and Tradition   11
   Where Pots can be Seen   11

References   13

Illustrations and Catalogue   15
   Names in Jèrriais and English   17
   A Catalogue of Normandy Stoneware   31
      15th to mid 16th century   32
      Mostly 16th and 17th Century   34
      17th to early 18th Century   36
      17th or 18th century   38
      18th century   40
      18th century (cont.)   42

Acknowledgements   44

Normandy Stoneware

Large jug, 17th century. Found at Mont Orgueil in the Keep midden. Height: 32 cm.

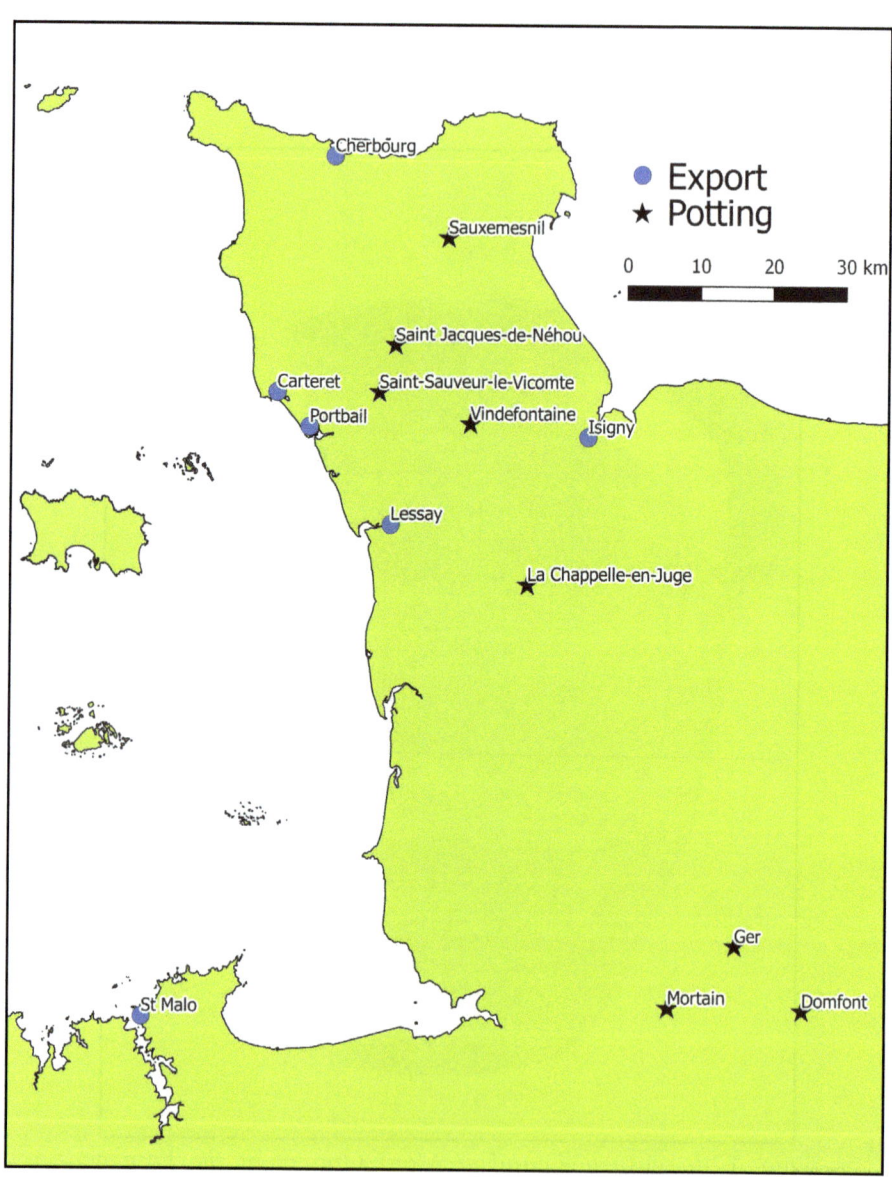

Normandy showing pottery centres and export points. (Source: Burns, 1991)

NORMANDY STONEWARE: AN INTRODUCTION

NORMANDY POTTERY

Stoneware pottery made in Normandy has been used in the Island for more than four hundred years. Dr Stéphen Chauvet, in his work *La Normandie Ancestrale*, described it as robust, rustic and traditional.

There was a pot made for every household purpose and the variety can be quite bewildering. Used on farms and in town houses alike, these were the forerunners of factory produced crockery. Nevertheless they proved sufficiently durable and practical to continue in use well into the 20th century. Nowadays, the pots may still be found in farm lofts or as ornaments and some types could still be bought from Le Lievre's ironmongers shop in Queen Street, St Helier, in the 1920s.

They have become so much a part of Jersey's life that they might be described as Jersey pots although they have their exact counterparts in Normandy.

THE NATURE OF STONEWARE

Stoneware is a type of pottery produced when its clay has been fired to a sufficiently high temperature to produce vitrification. This makes it hard, waterproof and easy to clean.

In Normandy no differentiation used to be made between the terms earthenware and stoneware so these pots were described as *terre cuite* or baked clay but now they are more commonly known as *grès normands*. In the *Dictionnaire Jersisais-Français* they are called *vide terr'rie*. The names given in this book are all in Jèrriais (Jersey Norman-French).

No kiln or record of production of this type of pottery has been discovered in Jersey. It is not surprising as the natural materials required have never existed here in sufficient quantities. The major challenge was the supply of wood in the form of forest trees for fuelling the kilns as well as sufficient clay and running water.

Stoneware was, however, made throughout the Cotentin peninsula. The most important centres for the Channel Islands were probably Sauxemesnil, Vindefontaine and Saint Jacques-de-Néhou. Knowledge of how to make stoneware is likely to have reached Normandy from the many production areas of the Rhineland.

A HISTORY OF PRODUCTION

In 1831, the Abbé Lebredonchel wrote in his history of the parish of Néhou of the long tradition of pottery making in the area, beginning with the evidence for kilns from the Gallo-Roman period. He mentions a document dated 1223 which recorded the construction of three kilns.

By the 16th century there was a well-established industry and by the

Workshop of the pottery at Saint Jacques-de-Néhou near Carteret at the beginning of the 20th century. (La Normandie Pittoresque, no. 2454: reproduced with permission from M. Le Goubey)

early 19th century numerous kilns worked in and around the town. According to Dr Chauvet, during the period 1820-1827 some 203,370 kg of pots were exported to the Channel Islands through the ports of Portbail and Carteret.

Quantities were also sent to the annual fair at Lessay which is still frequented by Jersey people. In Saint Jacques-de-Néhou, potter Pierre Hamel worked until 1920 and was succeeded by his son, Pierre. The last potter there was Alphonse Hamel who died in 1977.

THE APPEARANCE OF THE POTTERY

A basic difference can be detected between the fabrics of the north-west and those of the south-west of Normandy. Both have changed little over the centuries. Bessin ware, the name given to the productions of the north, is an overall dark plum or plum-brown colour with partial shoulder glazing often occurring when salt was thrown into the kiln at the time of firing. Ash from the kiln also altered the appearance of the surface in a similar way to salt.

Later, lead glazing became common and required a second firing. Although some of the pots of the south can be a brown colour, those particularly of the Domfront and Ger districts of the Orne have a grey or grey-black, sometimes rough surface and the fabric is a pale tan or butterscotch colour (Dufournier and Fajal, 1990).

POTTERY MARKS AND STAMPS

Stamped Initials

Potters marks have been recorded in Jersey on a number of occasions. Usually, they occur on tall jars, under the rim and close to the handle, but recently the inscription 'Sauveur-le-Vicomte' was found under the spout of a broken jug. It is likely that all those which include the letter 'V' are from the kilns at Saint-Sauveur-le-Vicomte. Initials found to date are J.V., P.I. and F.T.

Stamped Patterns

Stamped patterns are marks on a pitcher or container, usually over the handle. A number of kiln sites are known to have produced pots to hold butter which was exported widely, including to Canada. (Décarie-Audet, 1979).

Stamps of different patterns have been found during excavations in Normandy and Brittany (Langouët et Regnault, 1983). All the vessels appear to be of similar size and form and it would seem certain that these were made for the export of butter or honey and that the stamp was an assurance of quality, good measure and place of origin. Such a stamped sherd was found at Mont Orgueil during Major Rybot's investigations in the 1930s. It has a mark most closely resembling one from a similar-sized vessel uncovered in Rouen.

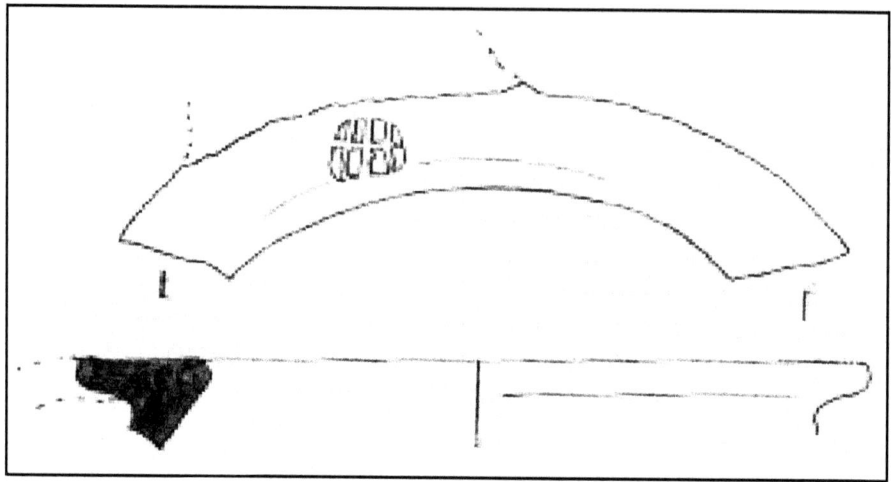

Pottery stamp on a jar from Mont Orgueil.

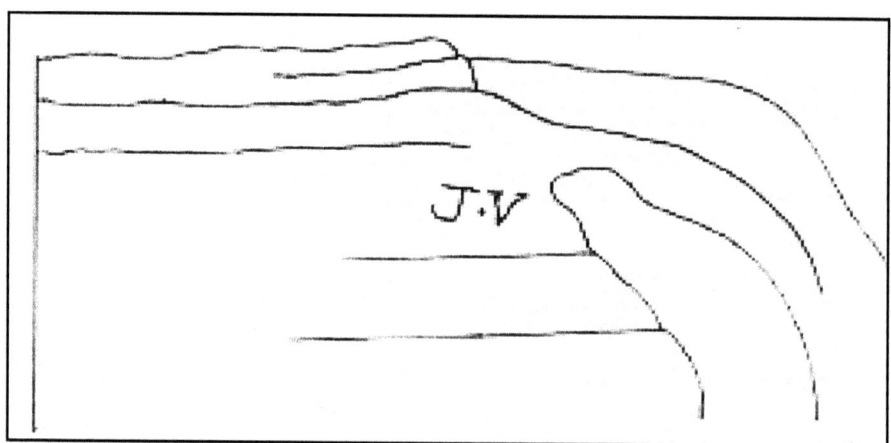

Initials from Saint-Sauveur-le-Vicomte.

DATING AND TRADITION

So far, archaeology has established that the earliest Normandy stone ware found in both Jersey and Guernsey dates to the fourth or fifth decades of the 15th century. It was a transformation from the earlier medieval hard-fired earthenware made in the Cotentin peninsula known as Normandy Gritty Ware and which ended finally in a brief, developed form in the late 14th and early 15th centuries.

The occasional reintroduction of successful designs in later centuries and the unchanging nature of the fabric over time have often made the dating of individual pots difficult. Some vessels can certainly be called traditional, such as the bottle (*eune bûsette*) and the jug (*eune jougue*), both in use at least since the 18th century. The large salting crock (*un saleux*), used for preserving food such as pork or fish, is also common in a number of forms.

The fine and unusual terrine (*un chanmeau*) is described by Dr Chauvet as decorated with a hare attacked by ermine (stoats) and as a rarity in Normandy. They are known to have been made in Sauxemesnil, some inscribed with dates in the second half of the 18th century. The Société Jersiaise has two examples. Two other charming pieces are the *chaufferette* (*un chaûffe-pid*) or foot-warmer and a jug converted either for use as a lantern, or for raising pigeons.

It is noticeable that some pots, principally the *hanapés*, are often marked by burning on one side, indicating the custom of pushing them into the ashes at the edge of the hearth so as to warm the contents.

WHERE THE POTS CAN BE SEEN

In Jersey, the Société Jersiaise has a fine collection as part of its Agricultural Heritage material which it is hoped will go on display again soon. From time to time there is also a display at the Hamptonne Rural Life Museum. Amongst places in Normandy there is a good general display at the Musée de Normandie at Caen, another in the Arts and Traditions section of the Musée. Quesnel-Morinière in Coutances and at Ger in Lower Normandy, where there are also restored kilns.

Decorated roof ridge tiles and finials, often in the form of cavaliers or horsemen, were also made but have yet to be identified in the Channel Islands. In Guernsey and Alderney, horsemen finials are to be seen on roof tops but these are very weathered and are considered to come from England.

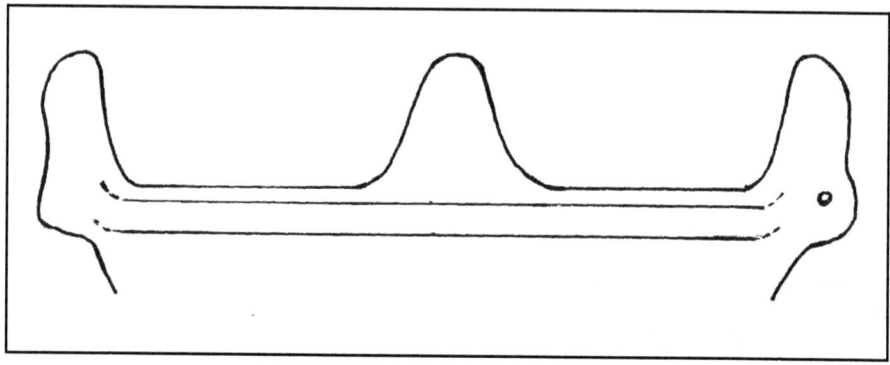

Bowl from a chafing dish or food warmer for the table. Late 15th to early 16th century. Excavated at Hamptonne Farm. Width: 24 cm.

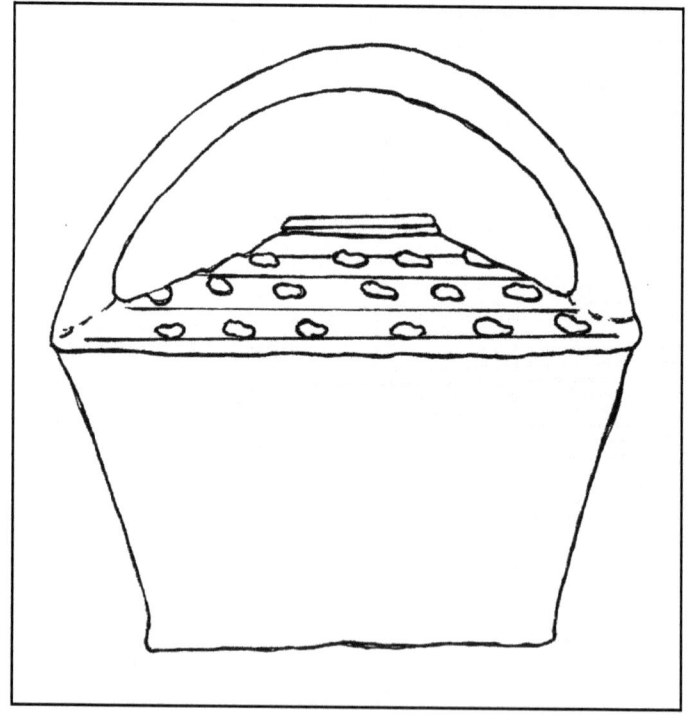

Un chaûffe-pid (footwarmer). In private ownership. Height: 20 cm.

REFERENCES

Burns, R. (1991), 'Post Medieval Normandy stonewares from Guernsey', in *Custom and Ceramics: essays presented to Kenneth Barton*. Wickham: APE, pp 104-127.

Chauvet, S. (1950), *La Normandie ancestrale*. Bayeux: R. P. Collas.

Décarie-Audet, L. (1979), *Les Collections archéologiques de Place Royale: le grès français*. Québec: Ministère des Affaires Culturelles.

Dufournier, D., & Fajal, B. (1990). 'Céramologie et aspects de l'artisanat potier dans l'Orne', in *Empreines, l'Orne archéologique*, catalogue d'exposition, Alençon, pp 86-90.

Finlaison, M. (1998), 'A group of Normandy stonewares of the second half of the 15th century, Hamptonne Farm, Jersey', in *Guernsey Connections: archaeological and historical papers in honour of Bob Burns*, ed. H. Sebire. Guernsey: La Société Guernesiaise, pp 108-111.

Langouët, L. (1983), 'Les grès Normands retrouvés dans les fouilles sous-marines de la rade de Solidor à Saint-Malo', in *Les Dossiers du Centre Régional Archéologique d'Alet*, no. 11.

Langouët, L., & Regnault, C. (1983), 'Sur des Mercs de Potiers Normands et Bretons', in *Les Dossiers du Centre Régional Archéologique d'Alet*, no. 11, pp 81-94.

Lebredonchel, M. (1855), *L'histoire de la paroisse de Néhou: depuis les temps les plus reculés jusqu'à nos jours*. Cherbourg: Noblet.

Le Goubey, J-B. & Veyssières, A. (1989), *Jean-Baptiste Le Goubey et Anet Veyssières : photographes en Cotentin (1900-1920)*. Cherbourg: Isoète.

Le Maistre, F. (1966), *Dictionnaire Jersiais-Français*. Jersey: Le Don Balleine.

Lepoittevin, L., Lebuerruyer, P. & Bonnet, A. (1983), *Poteries et céramiques anciennes du Cotentin*. Coutances: Arnaud-Bellé.

Rybot, N. V. L. (1930), 'Report on the reparations and investigations in Mont Orgueil Castle 1921-1929' *ABSJ* 11, pp 274-367.

Normandy Stoneware

ILLUSTRATIONS AND CATALOGUE

Terrine, un chanmeau. Mid to late 18th century. Height: 20 cm.

NAMES IN JÈRRIAIS AND ENGLISH

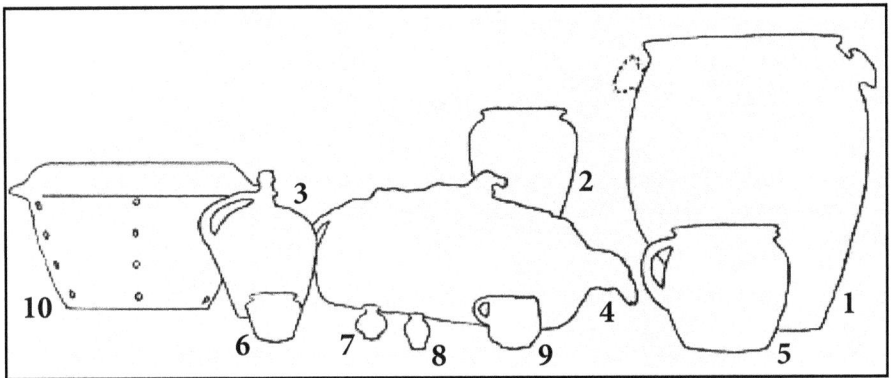

1 - UN SALEUX. A vessel for laying down salted pork.

2 - EUNE JARRE. A jar.

3 - EUNE JOUGUE. A jug.

4 - UN CHANMEAU. A decorated terrine.

5 - UN HANAPÉ À DEUX HANGNES. A vessel with two handles.

6 - EUNE P'TITE JARRE. A small jar for honey or preserves.

7 - EUNE P'TITE JOUGUE À PARFUM. A small perfume bottle.

8 - EUNE P'TITE JOUGUE À PARFUM. A small perfume bottle.

9 - UN HANA. A cup.

10 - UN COULEUX. A strainer.

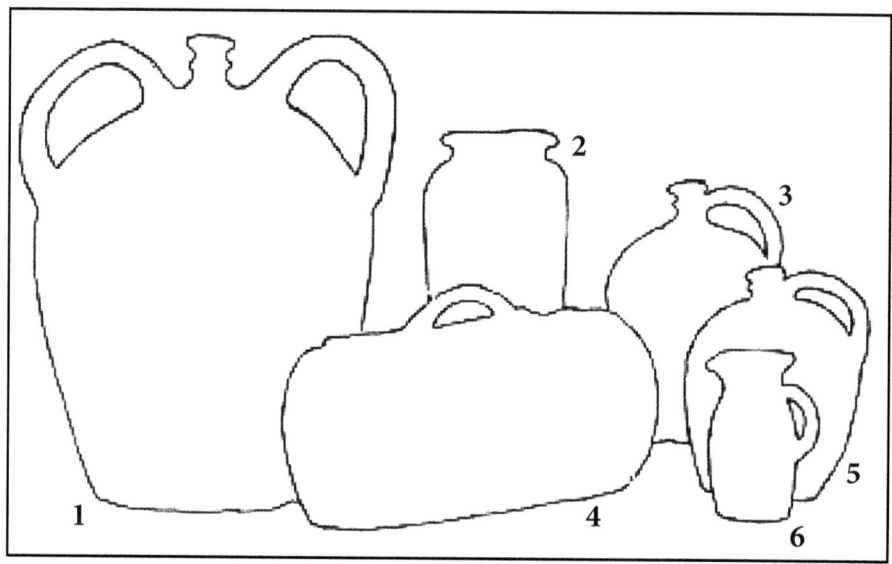

1 - EUNE DANME-JEANNE. A jar with two handles.

2 - EUNE JARRE À LANCHON. A jar for sand eels.

3 - EUNE JOUGUE. A jug.

4 - UN CHANMEAU. A casserole or terrine.

5 - EUNE JOUGUE. A jug.

6 - EUNE CANNE. A jug.

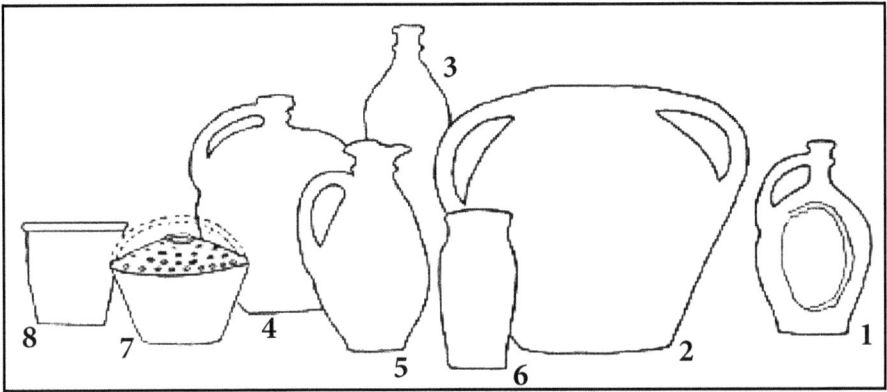

1 - EUNE JOUGUE. A jug adapted for use as a lantern, or a bird's nest for the eaves, 18th century.

2 - EUNE GRANDE JARRE. A large jar with two handles.

3 - EUNE BÛSETTE. A bottle for cider or wine.

4 - EUNE JOUGUE À CIDRE. A jug for cider.

5 - EUNE JOUGUE. A jug.

6 - UN POT À MYI OU À FLIEURS. A pot for honey or flowers.

7 - UN CHAÛFFE-PID. A foot warmer with handle missing.

8 - UN POT À FLIEURS. A flower pot.

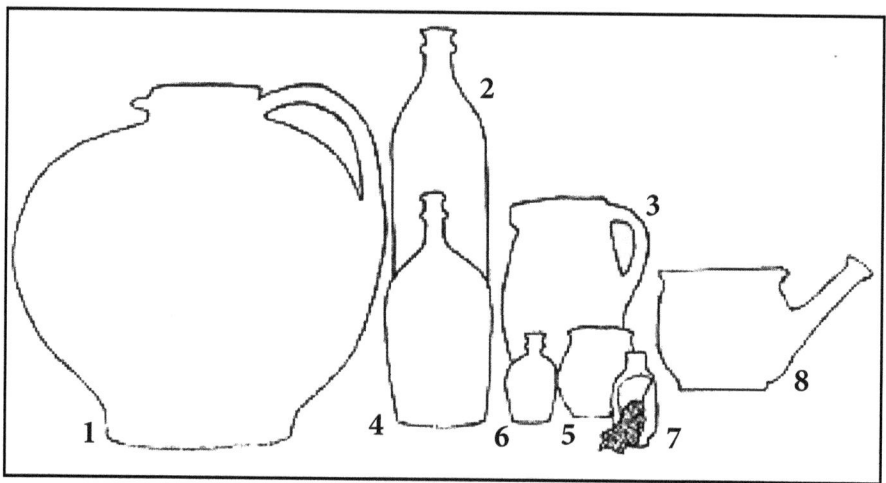

1 - EUNE GRANDE CANNE. A large jug.

2 - EUNE BÛSETTE. A bottle for cider or wine.

3 - UN HANAPÉ. A large cup for heating drinks at the fire.

4 - EUNE JOUGUE. A jug.

5 - EUNE P'TITE JARRE. A small Jar for honey or preserves such as jam and pickles.

6 - EUNE P'TITE JOUGUE À IEAU D'VIE. A small jug for spirits.

7 - EUNE P'TITE BÛSETTE. A small bottle found during archaeological excavations in St Helier in the wall of a hearth and containing a hand sewn ribbon from a child's bonnet; thought to be a charm against whooping cough. Late 18th or early 19th century.

8 - STCHILET OR HANAPÉ. A small long handled cooking pot.

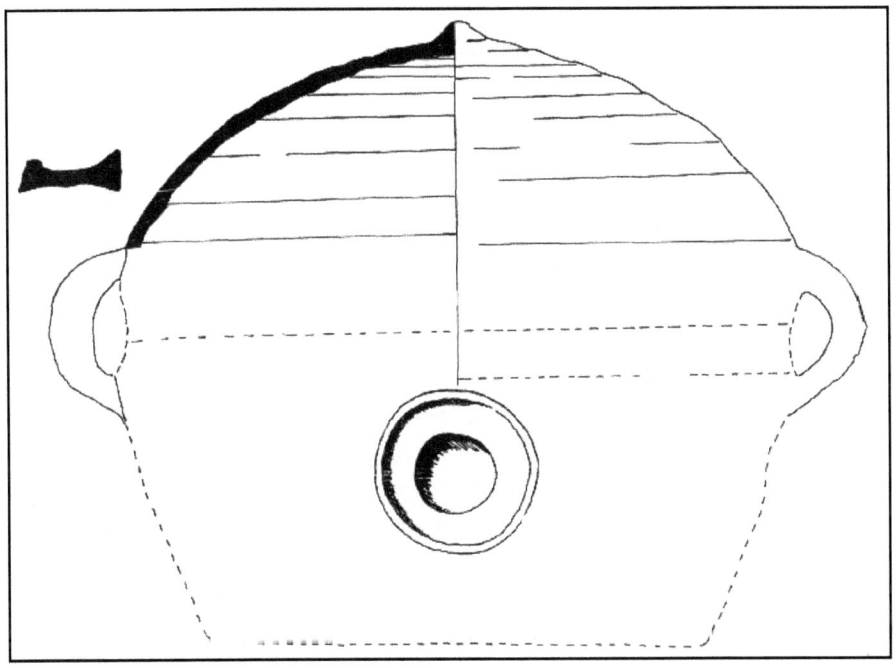

Costrel or jug for taking drink to the fields. Excavated at Hamptonne Farm. 1450-1550. Height: 24 cm.

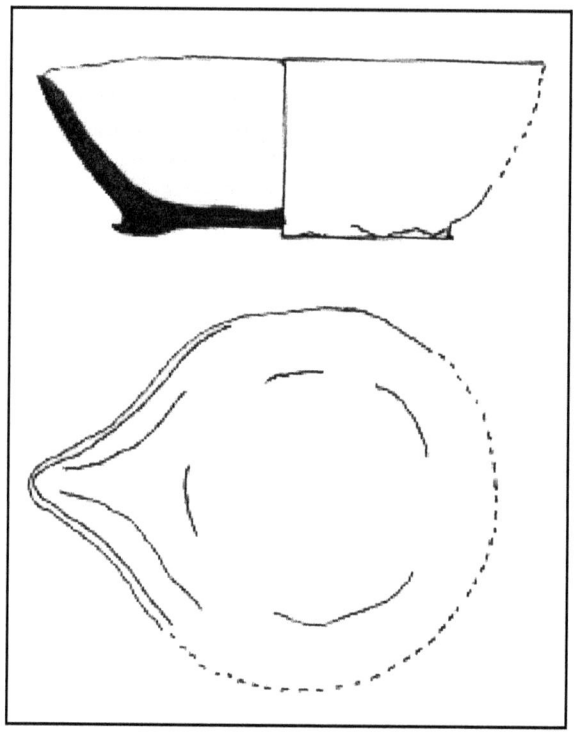

Part of a cresset or oil lamp, date unknown. From Mont Orgueil. Height: 5 cm.

1 - JAR WITH TWO HANDLES
2 - MUG WITH TWO HANDLES
3 - JUGS
4 - JUGS
5 - JAR FOR SAND EELS
6 - DECORATED JUGS

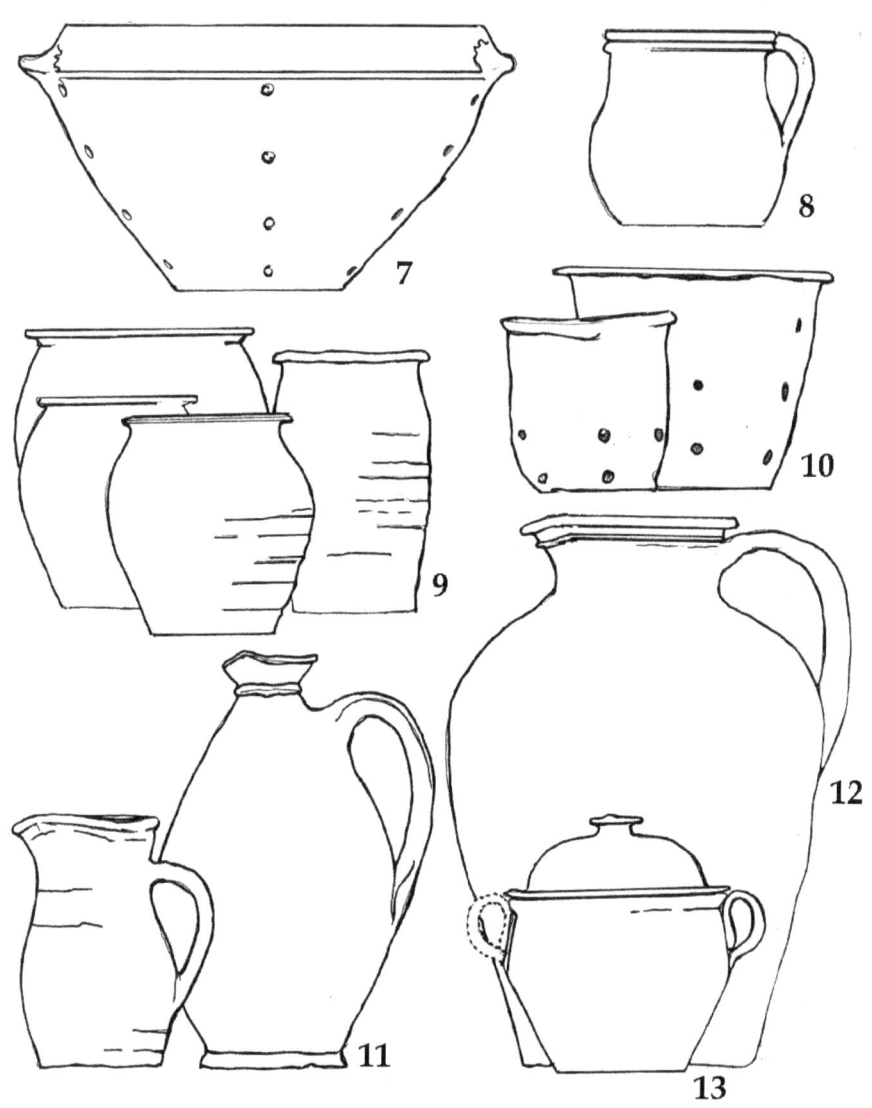

7 - STRAINER

8 - MUG

9 - JARS

10 - STRAINERS FOR CHEESE

11 - JUGS

12 - LONG JUG

13 - TRIPE JAR

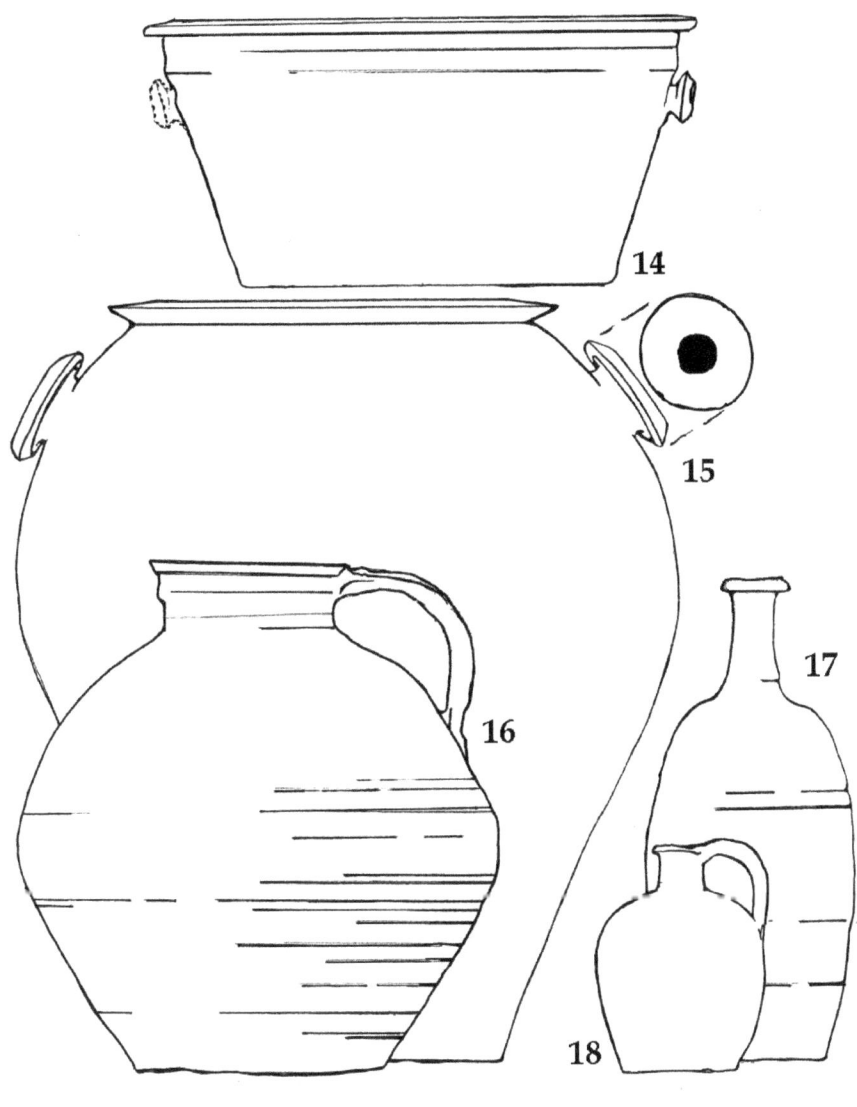

14 - MIXING BOWL OR CREAM PAN
15 - SALTING JAR
16 - LARGE JUG
17 - BOTTLE
18 - SMALL JUG

SMALL-HANDLED COOKING POT

BOTTLES

LARGE JARS

LARGE JUG. Height: 35 cm.

SALTING JAR. Height: 47 cm.

LARGE JUG WITH TWO HANDLES. Height: 30 cm.

JUG. Height: 20 cm.

JAR WITH TWO HANDLES.
Height: 16 cm.

MUG. Height: 10 cm.

JUG. Height: 24 cm.

JUG WITH HAND PAINTED DECORATION. Height: 10 cm.

CATALOGUE OF NORMANDY STONEWARE FROM RESCUE EXCAVATIONS IN ST HELIER: 1972-1994

15th to mid-16th CENTURY

This material is from the floors and yard surfaces of two buildings on the sites of 44 Don Street and 22-24 Hue Street.

Dating is taken from a sealed pit group at Hamptonne Farm and dated sealed groups at Castle Cornet, Guernsey (Burns, 1991). Found in association with Normandy buff-coloured earthenware, Breton coarse brown ware and Beauvais stoneware from Picardy. All are Bessin wares with the exception of No. 1 which is Domfront.

1 - Jug with cupped rim and shoulder shelf. 1400-1450.

2 to 5 - Jug rims with cupped necks. 15th century.

6 - Small Jar. 1450-1500.

7 - Rim. 15th century.

8 - Rim. *Circa* 1550.

9, 10 - Two jug rims. *Circa* 1550.

11 - Jug neck with handle scar. Pale orange-red fabric and grey surfaces. *Circa* 1550.

12 - Jug with grooved neck, fabric as no. 11. 1450-1500.

13 - Jug neck. *Circa* 1550.

14 - Handle. *Circa* 1550.

15 - Large jar, fabric as no. 12. 15th century.

16 - Jar rim. 1400-1450.

17 - Large crock with grooved rim. Late 15th century.

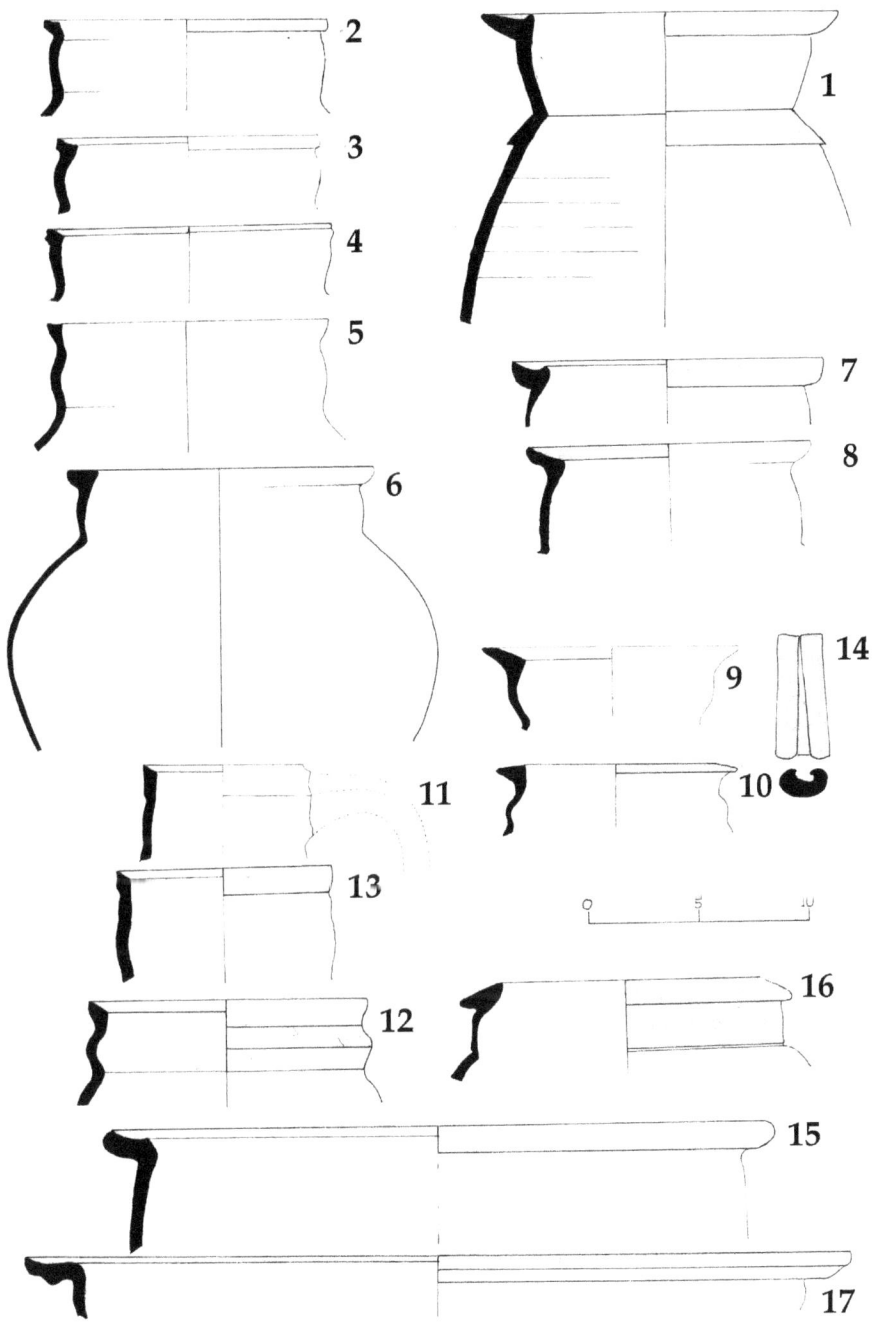

MOSTLY 16th AND 17th CENTURY

From Don Street, Hue Street and King Street. Dated again from the previous groups.

All are Bessin wares with the exception of 18, 22, 23, which are from Domfront.

18 - Cup-necked jug rim. Mid 15th-early 16th century.

19 - Finely rilled jug neck. Probably 17th century.

20 - Cupped jug rim with shoulder shelf. Late 16th to early 17th century.

21, 22 - Two ridged strap handles. Both probably associated with the jugs above.

23 - Cup-shaped jug rim. Mid-late 16th century.

24 - Cup-shaped jug rim. Mid-late 16th century.

25 - Flat jug rim. Grey outer and orange-red internal surface and core. 16th century.

26 - Flanged jar. Mid–late 16th century.

27 - Large flanged jar. Mid–late 16th century.

28 - Base with feet, probably jug. *Circa* mid 17th century.

29 to 33 - Five bases. All 15th-16th century.

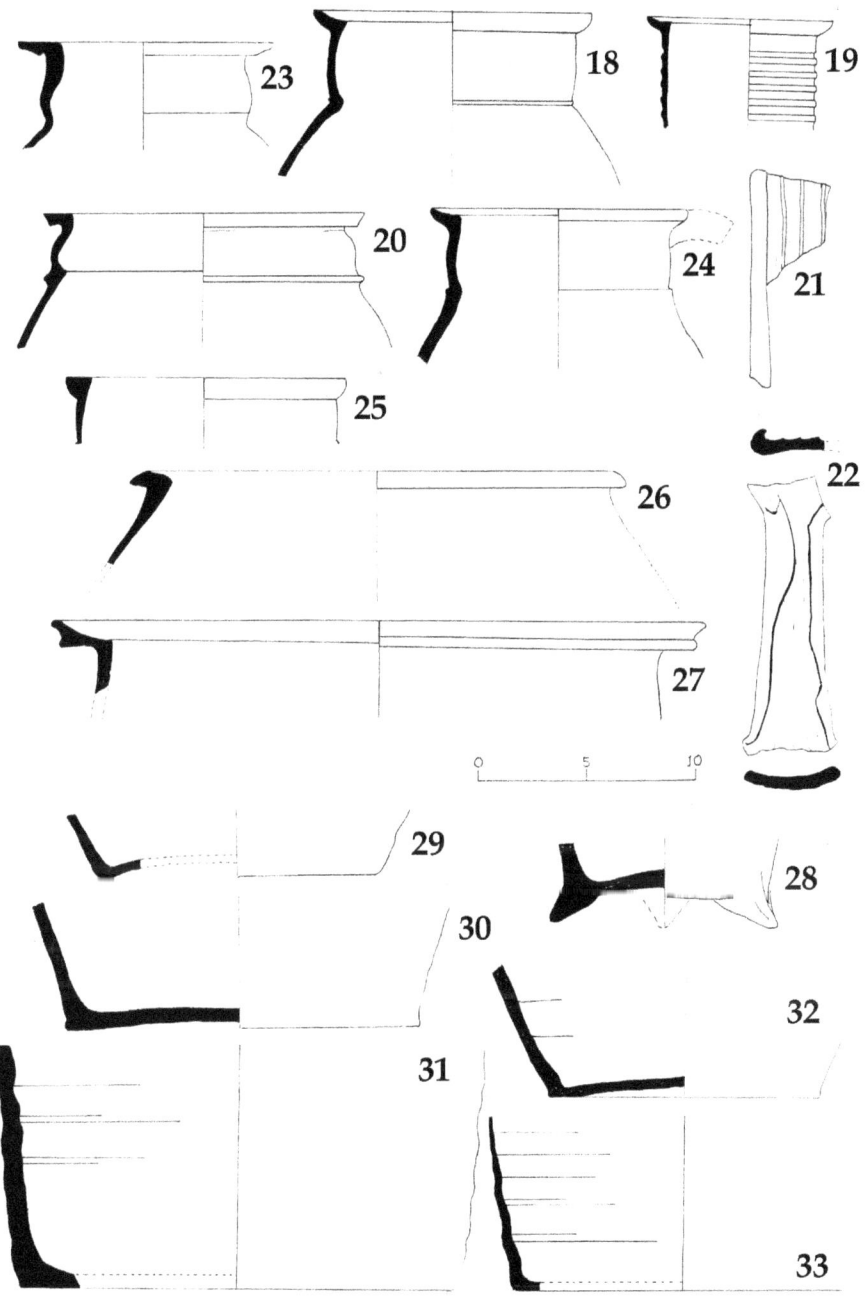

17th TO EARLY 18th CENTURY

These vessels are again principally from sites in Don Street, Hue Street and Old Street and most are comparable with Burns group 6. Found in association with Beauvais stoneware and Dutch tin-glazed earthenware.

All are Bessin ware with the exceptions of numbers 37, 40 and 45 which are Domfront.

34 - Lid with thumbed decoration. Late 17th to early 18th century.

35 - Bowl from the upper half of a chafing dish. 1680-1700.

36 - Jug with rod handle. Late 17th-early 18th century.

37 - Jug with solid rod handle. *Circa* 1650.

38 to 44 - Jug necks. Late 17th-early 18th century.

45 - Flanged jar. Late 17th-early 18th century.

46 to 48 - Flanged jars. Probably 17th century.

49 - Flanged dish. Late 17th-early 18th century.

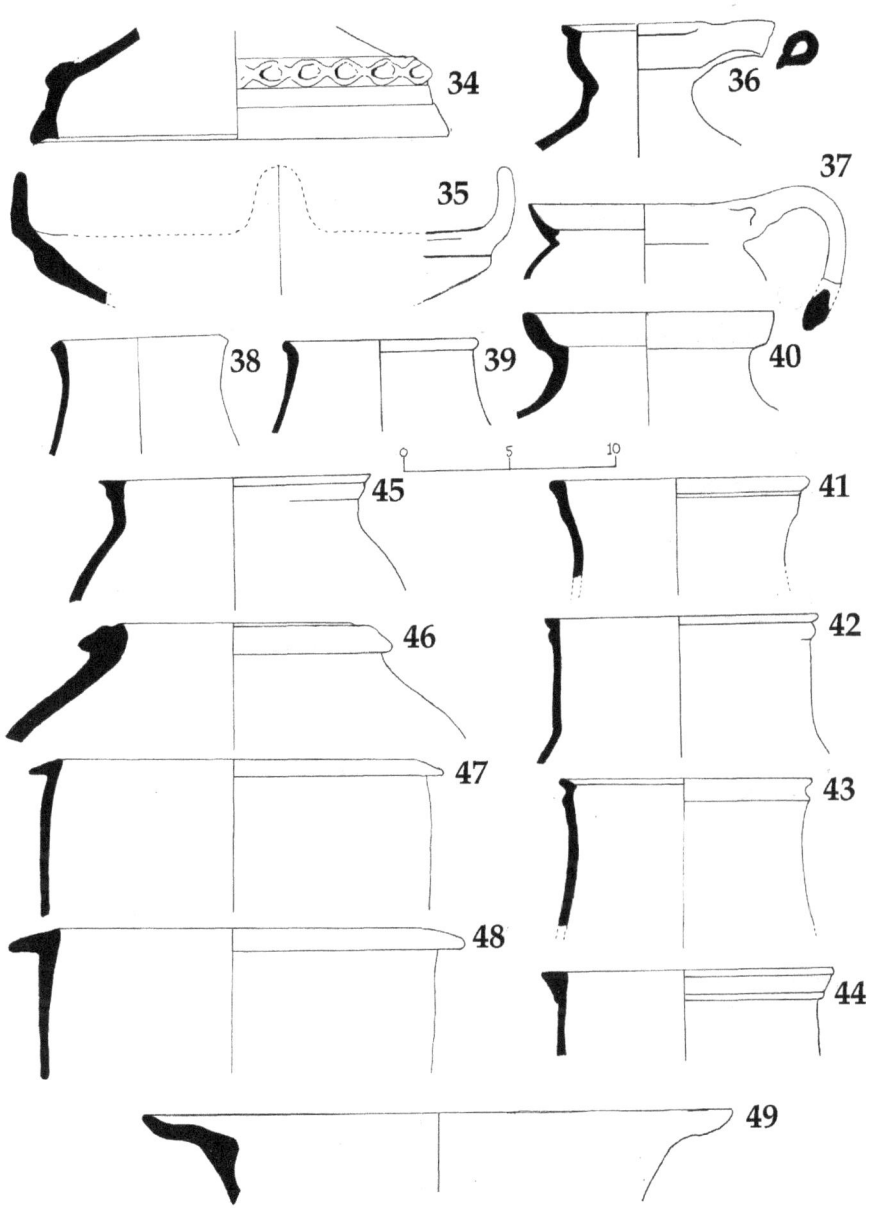

17th OR 18th CENTURY

All are Bessin ware except 61 which is from Domfront.

- 50 - Bucket pot. Unstratified. Probably 18th century.
- 51 - Jug neck. Early-mid 18th century.
- 52 to 54 - Jug necks. 18th century.
- 55 - Pot neck with stub of solid rod handle. Unstratified. Probably 18th century.
- 56 - Similar to before. Unstratified. Probably 18th century.
- 57 - Handled jar or pot. Unstratified. Probably 18th century.
- 58 - Base. 18th century.
- 59 - Flanged bowl. Unstratified. Probably 18th century.
- 60 - One- or two-handled jar. Early-mid 18th century.
- 61 - Tall jar. 17th or 18th century.

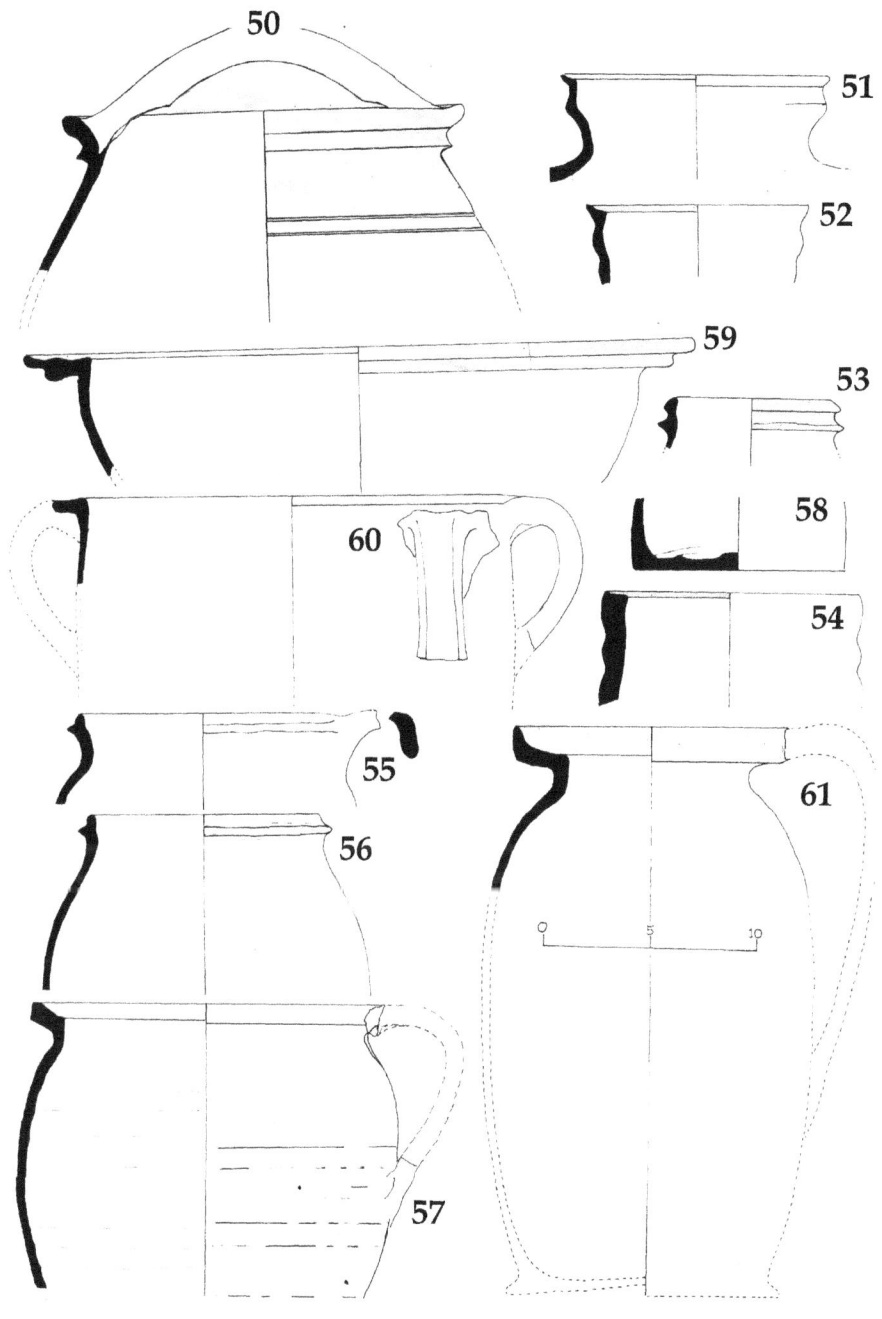

18th CENTURY

From a wide number of sites.

During this time, in addition to utilitarian wares, many well-made items such as small bottles were produced, and jugs suitable for the dinner table.

Associated finds include Westerwald stoneware mugs with AR and GR royal initials, Staffordshire combed and trailed slipware dishes and slipware from Martincamp, Seine-Maritime, Normandy. From the mid-later 18th century English white salt-glazed stoneware and English creamware and Italian Albisola black banded dishes, numbers 62-77 and 89 are from Domfront/Ger. Numbers 78-82 are Bessin ware.

> 62-73 - A series of small bottles and jars perhaps for scent or cordial Late 17th and early 18th century.
>
> 74-77 - Albarelli or unguent jars. Late 17th and early 18th century.
>
> 78-80 - Jars and containers.
>
> 81 - Jar with pulled lip. 17th-18th century.
>
> 82 - Jug adapted for use as a lantern or pigeon nest. Jug date unknown, a very long-standing design. Société Jersiaise collection.

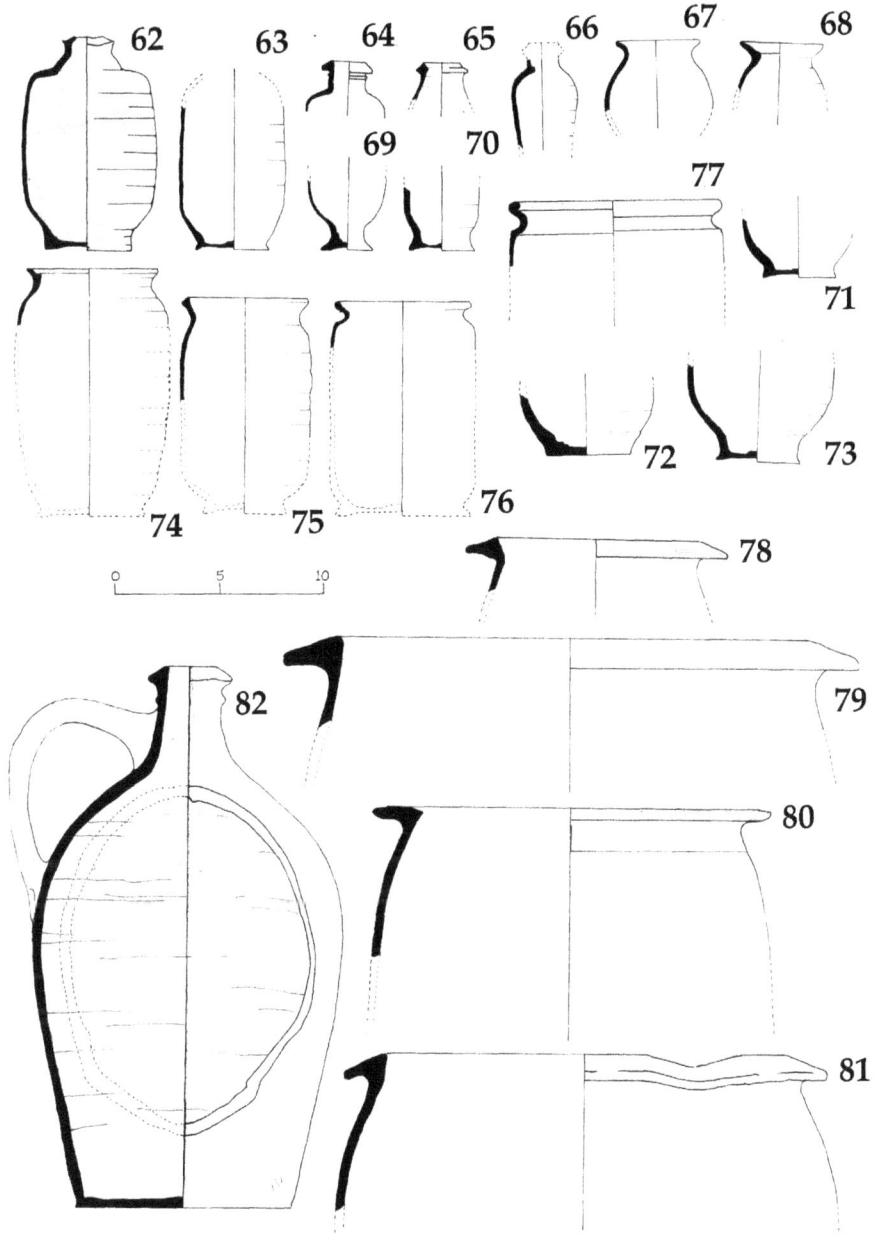

18th CENTURY (cont.)

83-87 - Small jugs.

88 - Small flower pot.

89 - Tall storage or salting jar.

90 - Large storage jar.

91-92 - Two small jug spouts.

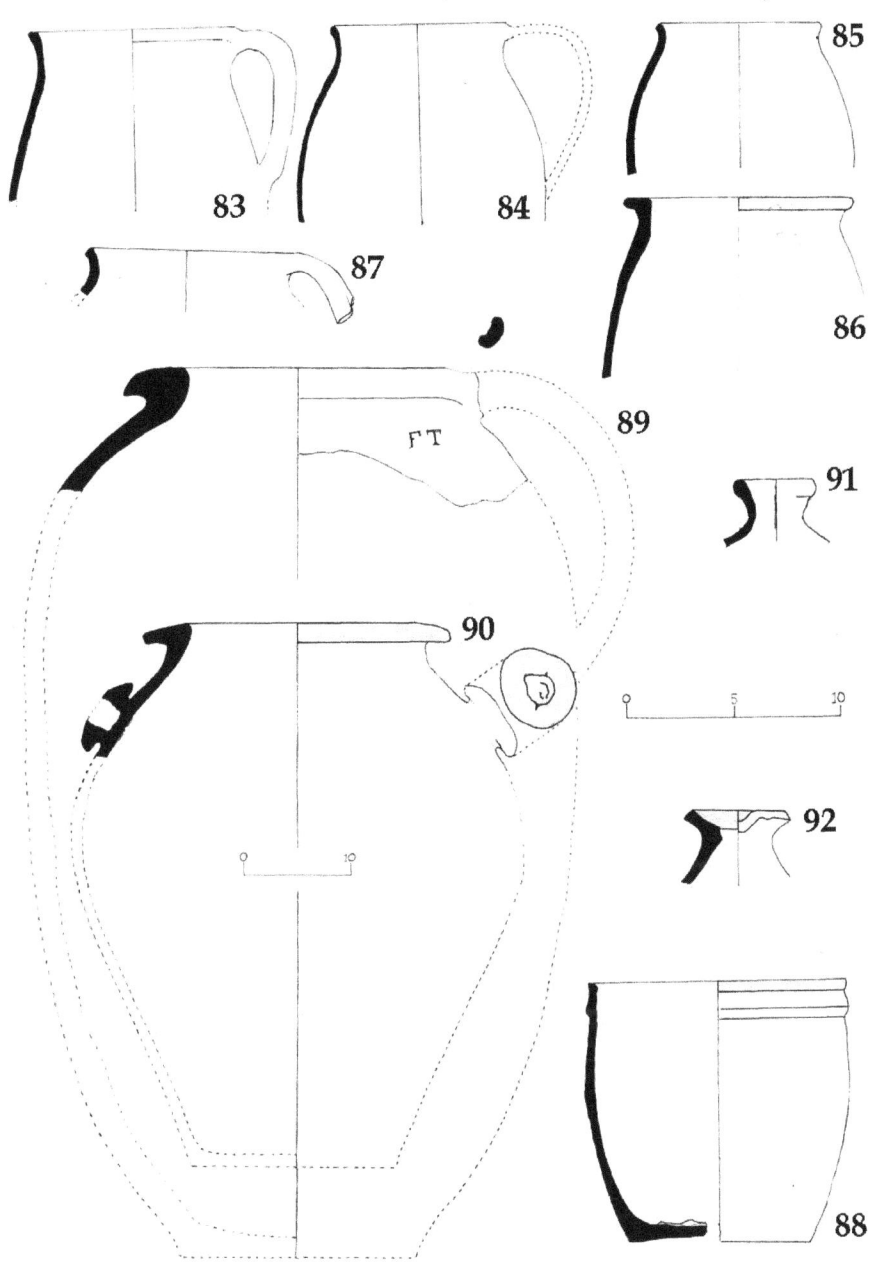

ACKNOWLEDGEMENTS

This record owes a great deal to the enthusiasm and contribution of the late Dr Frank Le Maistre whose valuable assistance is acknowledged here. In the 1970s when this recording began, he was able to name the pots in Jèrriais in his parish of St Ouen and the uses to which they had been put. It should be mentioned that name differences occur across the Island, but this remains the most complete parish record we have.

The Committee from the Section de la Langue Jèrriaise of the Société Jersiaise, has made a valuable contribution in the interpretation of the Jèrriais names.

The comprehensive research undertaken by past Guernsey Archaeology Curator, Bob Burns, in his report on the stoneware in Guernsey, has frequently been drawn upon here and it remains the most complete history so far published for the Channel Islands.

My especial thanks go to John de Carteret and Neil Mahrer for their photography of much of the collection of the Société Jersiaise, and to Ann Spencer for assistance with the drawing and permission to reproduce her profile drawings taken from a past exhibition by the Archaeology Section.

I am especially grateful to Janine Aubin for her patient production of the text and to Paul Chambers, Clare Cornick, Roger Long, Bronwyn Matthews, Neil Molyneux, John Noel and other members of the Société Jersiaise for their assistance with proofing and designing the final publication.

Margaret Finlaison

Normandy Stoneware

www.ingramcontent.com/pod-product-compliance
Ingram Content Group UK Ltd.
Pitfield, Milton Keynes, MK11 3LW, UK
UKHW022120230426
12048UKWH00010BA/615